The Prosperity Handbook

WINNING THE MONEY GAME

Gower

THE
PROSPERITY
HANDBOOK
WINNING THE MONEY GAME

Paul de Haas and Surya Lovejoy

Published by
Gower Publishing Limited   Gower
Gower House   Old Post Road
Croft Road   Brookfield
Aldershot   Vermont 05036
Hampshire GU11 3HR   USA
England

Surya Lovejoy and Paul de Haas have asserted their right
under the Copyright, Designs and Patents Act 1988 to be
identified as the authors of this work.

British Library Cataloguing in Publication Data

Haas, Paul de
  Prosperity Handbook: Winning the Money
  Game
  I. Title   II. Lovejoy, Surya
  332.024

  ISBN 0-566-07447-8

Library of Congress Cataloging-in-Publication Data

De Haas, Paul, 1945–
    The prosperity handbook: winning the money game / by Paul de Haas
  & Surya Lovejoy.
        p.   cm.
    Published simultaneously in Great Britain.
    ISBN 0-566-07447-8
    1. Finance, Personal.   2. Wealth.   3. Financial security.
  I.Lovejoy, Surya.   II. Title.
  HG179.D375   1994
  332.024–dc20   93-48281
                                                               CIP

Typeset by Keyboard Services, Luton, and printed in
Great Britain by Hartnoll Ltd, Bodmin

■ DEDICATION ■

To my mother, Henny de Haas,
and my wife, Marian
PdH

To my wife, Caroline
SL

Contents

Acknowledgements

As I have been dealing with money since the age of seven, it is hard to determine who to acknowledge for what. It is my view that there is something to be learned from every interaction. I am, however, particularly grateful to the thousands of people who have participated with me in the courses I have conducted around the world. Their stories and contributions were often full of insight, frequently hilarious and always educational.

I thank my mother for teaching me that money has nothing to do with what a human being is worth.

My thanks go, also, to all the teachers, authors. consultants, professionals and speakers who have influenced my thinking by sharing their thoughts with me.

Most of all, I thank my wife, Marian, for her unwavering support and partnership in all my endeavours.

PdH

While I no longer earn my living exclusively from writing, this seems an appropriate time to look back and thank some of the people who have enabled me to enjoy a nine-year career as a journalist and author. I would like to thank my parents, Patrick and Rosemary, for giving me an early love of the written word; Jane Bird, for an opportunity to cut my journalistic teeth on such a prestigious title as *Personal Computer World*; Bruce Sawford, for hiring an absurdly young and inexperienced magazine editor; Robin Oliphant, for setting the ball rolling on what turned out to be the start of many challenging and enjoyable assignments; the numerous newspaper and magazine editors who made a freelance career rather more secure than is often the case; Richard, Ian, Fi, Brian, Dave, Jane and the rest of the top-floor, Evelyn House gang for a highly enjoyable introduction to the world of book publishing; Clem Jones, for several fascinating assignments and consistently enjoyable interviews; all the clients who made Plain English such a success; and Chris Simpson and Malcolm Stern of Gower, for what I hope is only the beginning of a long and profitable association.

SL

Preface

You're probably sceptical about the value of this book. We hope so. Because a blind acceptance of its philosophy or content would be as pointless as a blind dismissal. We urge you to judge it for yourself ... and the only way to do that is to put it to the test, in practice.

Here's the deal. The book makes three promises to you, in return for three promises *from* you.

The book promises that:

- you will experience a dramatically increased level of prosperity;
- you will discover the source of all financial problems, including your own; and
- you will develop new, empowering and effective ways of relating to the four facets of money: earning, spending, saving and investing.

What we ask of you in return is to:

- play full out
  (a half-hearted flirtation with the programme will be a waste of your time);
- complete all 42 steps, in sequence
  (each one is an integral part of the programme); and
- reserve judgement on the programme for 30 days after completing the final step.

If you accept the deal as fair, read on. If not, we offer just one money-related tip: save yourself the cost of the book – put or send it back now!

Introduction

The Prosperity Handbook is for anyone who wants to make more money than they now have, but it's not about making money.

The book is for anyone who wants a powerful new way to plan and manage their finances, but it's not about financial planning.

The book is for anyone who wants to learn about successful approaches to handling money, but it's not a money advice book.

In fact, it's not even really about money: it's about prosperity. Most of us don't distinguish between the two. We think that the answer to our financial problems and aspirations lies in having more money. *The Prosperity Handbook* argues that it doesn't.

Don't misunderstand us. We're not suggesting you reject material wealth. We believe that money is both necessary and a powerful tool for living the life we want. We recommend that you take steps to generate more money in your life. Indeed, some of the steps in this book are specifically designed to do just that. But more money *alone* is unlikely to give you an experience of prosperity: you'll simply take on bigger commitments and develop more expensive tastes. We've met multi-millionaires who do not feel prosperous.

Prosperity resides not in a particular sum of money, but rather in your relationship to money. And that's where *The Prosperity Handbook* makes its mark. If you follow the steps in the book, you will almost certainly acquire more money than you now have – in many cases, substantially more. It would be hard not to. But that's not where the real value lies. Whether you want to live happily on a small sum of money, or become a billionaire (and both are equally valid goals), the step-by-step programme contained in these pages will provide you with new levels of power, control and freedom in each of the four key ways of relating to money: earning, saving, spending and investing.

■ 1 ■

The money genie

■ **Imagine a money genie has materialized before your eyes.**

Unlike the more conventional sort of genie, the money genie can grant only one wish, and it has to be money. You can, however, ask for as much money as you like. The money genie will provide you with any single sum: ten thousand pounds ... a hundred thousand ... a million ... ten million ... without limit.

There's just one condition: the amount of money you choose has to be a sum that makes sense to you. It must have some meaning to you. It is not enough to know how many zeroes it has. You must be able to conceive it as a real sum of money. You can't, for example, choose a googol anything – not even lira! You may know how many zeroes that has (a hundred, in case you're curious), but nobody can imagine such a sum of money.

So ... choose any sum you like, provided that you can picture the sum in your bank account. This amount will take care of you for the rest of your life. It will enable you to have, do or be anything you like. It includes investments, grants, donations, trust funds for your children . . . absolutely everything. Write that amount here:

£

Now, here's where the fun starts. Imagine that the money genie has waved its wand, clicked its fingers, chanted the magic words, or whatever it is genies do these days, and the money is now sitting in your bank account.

You go to the nearest cash machine, ask for an account balance and there it is on the screen, waiting for you. You own it. It's yours, to spend as you like.

Your job now is to decide how you would spend the money. Not what you *could* do with such an amount, nor what you *might* do with it if you felt like it at the time, but what you actually *would* do with it if it were sitting in your bank account right now.

You can buy anything you want, goods and services. You can travel anywhere. Set up charitable foundations. Give away money to your friends and family. Have homes all over the world. Buy your dream car. Give money away in the street. Put a sum aside in a reserve account. Anything you like.

Use Figure 1 on the following two pages to make a complete list of everything you would buy and do (ignore things you already buy and do). Alongside each item, put the approximate cost of the item. If you don't know, look it up or guess, but don't leave it blank. For example, *Travel around the world First Class for one year – £300,000.* Remember to include all your gifts, grants, donations and so on, together with an amount for each.

Do this now. Remember, this is how you actually *would* spend the money. You may continue on sheets of blank paper if you need more space.

When you've finished, add up the total amount you have spent.

Item	Approx. cost

Figure 1

Item	Approx. cost

Figure 1 Continued

You may find that you didn't ask for enough money to buy everything you wanted. You may find that you didn't come close to spending all the money you asked for. You may even find that you could buy everything on your list for a surprisingly small sum of money. Any of these outcomes will give you extra clues to your relationship to money.

But that's not the main purpose of this first step. Its purpose is to bring us one stage closer to reality: we don't want money, we want what money makes possible. Whether we want possessions, experiences or to change the world, money is merely the mechanism. What we want is what we can do with the money. And even that is only half the story, as you'll see later in the book. . . .

■ 2 ■

Getting the most from this book

■ **Never believe anyone's opinions about money.**

Every now and then, a millionaire writes a book telling everyone 'the secret to their success'. Some of these books do very well, selling 50,000 or more copies. Of those 50,000 readers, a handful will make a lot of money after reading the book.

Those handful of grateful readers will write glowing testimonials. The author will quote these in future advertisements, and another 50,000 people will buy the book. And so on.

No matter that, of any random selection of 50,000 people, a small minority will make a great deal of money irrespective of which books they read. No matter that you could replicate every action ever taken by the author and not make a bean. No matter that the vast majority of the readers don't make an extra penny. The books sell regardless.

There is, as far as we can tell, no secret of success; no magic formula; no reliable 'get rich quick' scheme. We therefore recommend that you view anyone's opinions on money as just that: opinions. Try them out, don't take them on trust.

■ Treat your own opinions in the same way

Our recommendation includes your own opinions. You almost certainly have opinions about money. For example: 'you have to have money to make money', 'money doesn't make you happy', 'you have to be selfish to be rich' and so on. You are also likely to have opinions about books on money. For example: 'they never make any difference', 'they might help some people, but not me', 'I'll probably make a bit more money by reading it, but not much' and so on. Since we ask you not to take on trust any opinions, including your own, you need to start by clarifying those opinions you already have.

■ Use Figure 2 to list all the opinions, beliefs and attitudes you have about money, and about books on money.

Remember, we don't ask you to reject any of these opinions, beliefs and attitudes. All we ask is that you view them *as opinions*.

This will be difficult. Most of us have plenty of 'evidence' to back up our views. We can cite countless examples of times when our opinions were borne out by events. We have 'proof'.

■ Try an experiment. Take any one of the beliefs you just listed. In the left-hand column of Figure 3, write down evidence which supports this opinion.
■ Now, play devil's advocate with yourself. Imagine that you want to find evidence to *disprove* the opinion. Think back through your life, and what you know of other people's experiences, and find exceptions to the rule. Write down in the right-hand column of Figure 3 all the evidence you can find that tends to argue *against* your opinion. Keep going until you have at least as much counter-evidence as you do evidence. Remember, we're not asking you to *change* your opinion, we merely want to clarify that it *is* an opinion.

Opinions, beliefs and attitudes about money

Figure 2

Opinions, beliefs and attitudes about money

Figure 2 Continued

Evidence *for* opinion	Evidence *against* opinion

Figure 3

It should be clear from this exercise that you could do the same thing with any of the opinions, beliefs and attitudes you listed in Figure 2.

We said earlier that we are not asking you to reject any of your opinions about money. That's true: we're not. But we *do* ask you to consider the possibility that they may not tell the whole story. Here's why:

We argue that your experience to date in the area of money is directly related to your knowledge, beliefs, opinions and attitudes about money. If this is true – and remember, it's just our opinion – then it may be necessary to experiment with some alternative viewpoints in order to experience a major financial breakthrough.

So here's what we ask: if anything in this book conflicts with your opinions, beliefs or attitudes – or even with things you consider to be facts – don't reject it, and don't accept it. Just consider the possibility that it may be useful to *act as if* our view were true.

Let's illustrate this with an example. Suppose you have an important meeting to get to, and you decide to travel by train. According to the timetable, the 08:30 train will get you there on time. Since it is vital to arrive on time, you may decide to catch an earlier train. It may not, in fact, be true that the service is unreliable, but you are choosing to *act as if* it were to ensure that you arrive punctually and to free you from the stress of worrying about delays.

That's all we ask in this book. By all means maintain your own beliefs and opinions. But – to get the most from the book – respond to any conflicting material by being willing, temporarily, to act as if it were true.

■ The 'little voice'

People's opinions are tenacious. They continually make themselves heard. It's as if we have a little voice in the back of our heads passing comment on everything we do, say and think.

That 'little voice' (the one now asking 'What little voice?') is adept at providing reasons for not trying out new ideas. It says 'no' far more readily than it says 'yes'. It is our own worst critic, and can often be our own worst enemy.

And it isn't even as if the opinions it voices are necessarily our own. Many – perhaps most – of the opinions it voices are those of our parents, our friends, our boss, the media ... even people we've overheard in the street.

■ Make a list in Figure 4 of all the self-defeating comments your 'little voice' has to make about you and money. For example: 'I don't know enough about money', 'No matter how much I earn, I never get ahead of the game', 'I'm too lazy to become rich', 'I'm in the wrong career to earn large sums of money' and so on.

Again, we don't ask you to reject or ignore your 'little voice'. The 'little voice' is simply a shorthand for a mixture of background thoughts and memories, many of which are very helpful. All we do ask is that you view its output in the same way as you would anyone else's: as interesting ideas, but not necessarily true.

■ Conclusion

Most 'getting the most from this book' sections are simple. They tell you to read this bit before that bit, to refer back to the summaries to refresh your memory, and so on. What we ask is very much harder. But it will need to be applied throughout the book if the programme is to make any real difference. As we said earlier:

We argue that your experience to date in the area of money is directly related to your knowledge, beliefs, opinions and attitudes about money. If this is true – and remember, it's just our opinion – then it may be necessary to experiment with some alternative viewpoints in order to experience a major financial breakthrough.

Self-defeating opinions about myself and money

Figure 4

One final point. Most of us make unconscious judgements about the relative value available to us from different types of material. If we pay £10,000 for a one-day course, we expect to obtain a great deal of value from that course. When we pay a few pounds for a book, we expect to get very much less value from it. We recommend that you do not allow the value you obtain from this book to be limited by the price you paid for it.

Some people have paid literally thousands of pounds for the material contained in this programme, and achieved results consistent with that. We suggest that you look for thousands of pounds' worth of value from this book, not a few pounds' worth.

Pick a sum of money that, if you had paid that much for the book, you would read it from cover to cover, completing every single step in full. Write that amount here:

£

Now act as if you really have paid that much. Be willing to let this book be the most powerful book you have ever read. It could be.

■ 3 ■

What is your personal net worth?

■ Establish your starting point.

Imagine that we are on board a boat somewhere in the middle of an ocean, and we want to sail to Venice. The very first thing we'd do is to find out exactly where we were now. Without that information, we wouldn't know how far we would have to go, how long it would take or even which direction we should take.

Similarly, it is very difficult to set and achieve meaningful financial goals until we know where we stand at present. And the most basic piece of information on our current position is our current personal net worth. This is the sum of all our assets and liabilities.

It's a basic piece of information for financial planning, yet most of us have no idea of our current net worth – not even whether it is a positive or negative figure! This third step thus provides a form for calculating your net worth.

Simply go through Figure 5 entering the appropriate figures. Some figures you will know immediately and with a high degree of accuracy. Some figures may require a little research (asking your

Assets	Amount
Cash in savings accounts	
Cash in current accounts	
Cash on hand	
Certificates of deposit	
Bonds (at today's value)	
Surrender value of life insurance policies	
Surrender value of annuities/endowments	
Surrender value of pension plan	
Surrender value of profit-share certificates	
Market value of home	
Market value of other property	
Market value of business interests	
Market value of stocks/shares/securities	
Market value of car(s)/other vehicle(s)	
Market value of household furnishings	
Market value of household appliances	
Market value of personal belongings	
Value of payments due to you (including tax)	
Other 1:	
Other 2:	
Other 3:	
Other 4:	
TOTAL VALUE OF ASSETS	

Figure 5

Liabilities	Amount
Current bills owing/anticipated (including tax)	
Overdraft(s)	
Credit/charge card balances	
Outstanding mortgage balance	
Outstanding balance on all other loans	
Other 1:	
Other 2:	
TOTAL LIABILITIES	

Figure 5 Continued

bank or accountant, for example), while a few may have to be estimated (for example, the current value of your personal belongings). Decide for yourself how much time you want to spend on obtaining accurate figures, but put in an estimate rather than leave an entry blank.

Those whose tax is deducted from their pay at source can normally ignore references to tax (unless you know that your tax situation is likely to change). Self-employed people will need to calculate the amount of tax due so far this tax year (plus any tax owing on earlier tax years).

Be honest. Nobody else need see these figures. The idea of this step is to give yourself a platform on which to stand when creating future goals. Lying to yourself is as self-defeating as pretending you're near Rhodes when you're really in Sydney Harbour – you may feel better, but your chances of reaching Venice are decidedly slim!

Once you have entered the values of all your assets, total them. Do the same with your total liabilities. Then subtract your total liabilities from your total assets to determine your current personal net worth. Write this figure here:

Personal net worth as of _____ (date): $+/-$ £_____

(Delete the plus or minus sign as appropriate.)

Don't be alarmed if your net worth is negative: this is true for a great many people. All you want from this step is a true picture of your current situation: changing it comes later.

■ 4 ■

What do you want to be worth?

■ Very few people become wealthy by accident.

Talk to most millionaires, and you will find that they had a specific financial goal they intended to achieve by a specific date. (As we will see in step 6, most millionaires became millionaires by failing to achieve these goals!)

There are exceptions, of course. Some people really are left unexpected fortunes by rich uncles. Some people do make millions from an idea they expected merely to pay a few bills. Some people do happen to be in the right place at the right time and make substantial sums of money almost in spite of themselves. And most of us like these stories: they appeal to the romantic in us. Sadly, however, these tales are the exception rather than the rule.

Some people don't like the idea of setting goals. They feel that goals make life too regimented, with too little room for spontaneity. Which is fine. You don't have to have goals. But the evidence suggests that, without them, you are unlikely to achieve a dramatic improvement in your financial circumstances. As the Chinese

Personal net worth goals by quarter		
Quarter	Date	Personal net worth goal
1		
2		
3		
4		
5		
6		
7		
8		

Figure 6

proverb says, if you don't know where you're going, you'll end up where you're headed. You have to decide which is more important to you: living a life free from goals, or achieving dramatic results.

You don't, of course, have to use the word 'goal'. Some of the people who find the word too restrictive prefer phrases like 'inspiring challenge'. Others, who find it too weak, prefer more solid-sounding words like 'objective'. Use whatever term works for you.

Use the form in Figure 6 to set personal net worth goals/challenges/ objectives, etc. for the next two years, quarter by quarter. You needn't yet know how you will achieve these goals. Don't worry too much at this stage about choosing the 'right' figures – we'll have more to say about them, and you'll have a chance to change them, in step 5. For the moment just put in figures which appeal to you and which are within the scope of what you believe to be *possible*, even if you have no idea how.

The first date should be approximately three months from today.

You may like to round up or down to make it the beginning or end of a month, or you may like to pick a date with particular significance to you – either practical significance (for example, a date when you are due to receive a particular sum of money) or emotional significance (for example, a wedding anniversary). The remaining dates should be at three-month intervals after that.

Write the dates in pen but the figures in pencil.

■ 5 ■

How much money do you want to make?

■ Make the game worth playing.

In step 4, you set goals for your net worth. We're now going to turn to income goals.

By 'income', we don't just mean a salary or personal drawings from a business, we mean *everything* which brings in cash and/or cash equivalents. This includes inheritances, prize wins, investment successes, gifts and so on. This may sound like a trivial distinction, but it is in fact key: the old saying that nobody ever got rich working for someone else may not be entirely true, but most people who make a great deal of money have discovered ways of breaking the link between hours worked and money made. We'll talk more about this in later steps, but for now, set your goals in terms of money *made*, not money *earned*.

One element of your income goals has already been decided in step 4. Given that you intend to improve your personal net worth by a certain amount each quarter, your income goals will have to at least cover this amount in addition to your day-to-day living expenses. For example, if you intend to jump from a net worth of £0 today to

£10,000 at the end of the first quarter, and your day-to-day living expenses are £1,500 a month (that is, £4,500 a quarter), then you'll need to make at least £14,500 in the first quarter, equal to an average of £4,834 a month. If you intend to have additional spending money available, you'll need to exceed this sum by the amount you want to have available to spend.

As before, you don't have to know yet how you will achieve your income goals: just set goals which are high enough to make it worthwhile investing some time and energy, while remaining within the bounds of what you consider *possible*. Note that we use the word 'possible' deliberately: you don't have to consider them *likely*.

Personal income goals by month for 19__ (year 1)		
#	Month/Year	Income goal
1		
2		
3		
4		
5		
6		
7		
8		
9		
10		
11		
12		

Figure 7

Personal income goals by month for 19___ (year 2)		
#	Month/Year	Income goal
1		
2		
3		
4		
5		
6		
7		
8		
9		
10		
11		
12		

Figure 7 Continued

And, as before, we'll have more to say about them in the following step.

Set down your income goals for the next two years in Figure 7. Again, write the dates in pen but the figures in pencil.

■ 6 ■

Expanding our vision (or 'failing big')

■ Most millionaires are failures.

They failed to achieve the goals they set themselves, and failed on a large enough scale – and frequently enough – to make a million. Instead of making ten million, they only made one. Instead of making a million, they made only £300,000. But most failed to achieve the goals they set themselves.

Most people who simply get by are, in contrast, successes. They set modest goals and achieve them. They set out to earn £20,000 one year, and do so. They aim for a salary rise of £2,000 and achieve it.

Most of us are so focused on 'success' that we rarely risk setting truly ambitious goals, goals we have no idea how to achieve. We set responsible goals. Realistic ones. Sensible ones. And we generally succeed. But what would you rather achieve: 100 per cent success at making £30,000, or only 10 per cent success at making a million?

Look back over the goals you set in steps 4 and 5. Ask yourself how you arrived at these goals. On what were they based? We'll make a safe bet: we bet they were based on a combination of your history and your present circumstances.

The German philosopher Arthur Schopenhauer said that we all 'take the limits of our own field of vision to be the limits of the world'. And our present field of vision is largely determined by our past experience.

History and circumstances are a perfectly sensible way to set safe, responsible, realistic goals. If you were about to take on financial commitments based on your goals, this would be the way to proceed. But this is a game. The money game. You are answerable to no-one if you fail: you risk only disappointment. And – if the goals are big enough, and you fail at a reasonable level – the disappointment shouldn't be too hard to bear.

For us, the whole point of a goal as a game is to generate sufficient interest and excitement such that you really want to play. If your goals don't excite you, they're too small.

This is not to say that you should slap in any old figure. Just as you can easily pick a figure that is too small to excite you, you can also pick one that is too big. If you pick a figure you think is utter nonsense, beyond even the wildest of possibilities, then it is unlikely to spur you to action. If you earned £20,000 last year, a goal of a billion pounds for next year isn't likely to be one you can seriously consider. But to go from £20,000 to £200,000 may be within the bounds of possibility. Enough people have made that type of leap. Pick figures that sound right to you, but make sure that the goals you set are neither too small to excite nor too big to encourage you to act.

Go back to steps 4 and 5 and review your quarterly net worth and monthly income goals. They are almost certainly too small. Increase them in line with the above test. Erase the pencilled figures and write the new ones in pen. These are the ones you will use.

■ 7 ■

What is your relationship to money?

■ What do you really think about money?

We said in the introduction that this book is designed to provide you with a new relationship to money, a relationship which provides you with new levels of power, control and freedom. And an essential part of achieving this is to become conscious of your *existing* relationship to money. Which is what this step is about.

We want you to make a list of every rule, thought, belief, idea, opinion, pattern and habit you have about money. Some of these will be immediately apparent to you. Others will be buried deeper and need a little coaxing into the light. Write these down in Figure 8.

Start with the ones you wrote down in step 2. Write these under whichever heading seems to fit best. If a particular thought, etc., seems to fit more than one heading, write it down under any of them. The headings aren't important: they're simply designed to prompt you.

When you find yourself stuck, think about any thoughts and behaviours you have while shopping for basics . . . shopping for treats

... paying bills ... paying off your credit or charge cards ... checking your bank statement ... paying money into your bank account ... paying money into a savings account ... drawing money out of a savings account ... applying for a loan ... receiving a gift of money ... making a gift of money....

Think about what your parents said to you about money when you were a child. Do you now agree with these views? Disagree with them? Very often, we end up either holding the same views on money as our parents, or adopting the exact opposite ones.

Write down as many things as you can think of. Spend at least 15 minutes on this step, but keep going if you're still thinking of things after that.

Now spend a little time reading through your list. This is your current relationship to money. You didn't choose it, it's just the one you

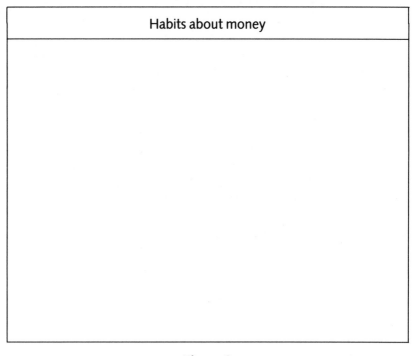

Figure 8

Rules about money

Thoughts about money

Figure 8 Continued

Opinions about money

Patterns about money

Figure 8 Continued

Beliefs about money

Ideas about money

Figure 8 Continued

picked up. Notice how much the things on that list influence your behaviour around money. The amount you earn, and how you earn it. The way you spend money, or don't. The way you save, or don't. The way you invest, or don't.

Step 9 will invite you to try out some new rules. In the meantime, add to your list of existing ones whenever you notice an additional one as you go through the rest of the book.

■ 8 ■

Where does money come from?

■ It's not what you think.

Where does money come from? Asked another way, what is it that people pay money for?

It's clearly not work, otherwise miners or hod carriers would be the richest people on earth.

It's not time, otherwise those who worked the longest hours would earn the most money.

It's not commitment, or dedication: some of the most dedicated people work in some of the lowest-paid jobs.

It's not intelligence: many of the brightest people work in academic institutions, not noted for their high salaries.

It's not material goods, otherwise mini-skirts would be much cheaper than maxi-skirts.

It's something far simpler than any of these things . . .

Ideas.

All money, ultimately, comes from ideas. In buying this book, you're not paying for the paper or the ink. You're not paying for the effort we put into it, the time we spent writing it, the commitment we have to it ... you're paying for the ideas it contains.

When you buy a suit or dress, you're not paying for the material used, or the time taken to make it, you're paying for the design – which is why mini-skirts cost just as much as maxi-skirts.

The materials, the construction, the work – all these may be *necessary*, but they are merely what is required to realize the idea. It is the idea you are buying. The manufacturer could change the design or construction of the product; change its employees; halve its costs; double its productivity rates; make any number of changes. But, as long as the product itself still looked and performed like the original, the customers would have no interest in these changes. The customers are buying the idea. And it is those who own the ideas who make the most money from the product or service, not those who perform the work.

You have probably come across 'Pet Rocks'. These were the brainchild of an American who considered that pets were fun, but required too much care. He had the idea of a pet which required absolutely no care whatsoever: a pet rock. He put a rock in a box with an ownership certificate, and sold them. Lots of them. He made $2.6 million in the first year.

People were not buying rocks. Rocks can be found lying around on the ground almost anywhere. People were buying *the idea* of a pet rock.

The Hula-Hoop, a simple plastic ring with a tiny production cost, made $800 million. People were not buying plastic: they were buying the idea of a hula-hoop.

Money itself is an idea. Once upon a time, people bartered goods. This worked in its way, but people soon realized that it was not particularly convenient. If you made cooking pots and wanted shoes, you would have to find a shoe-maker who happened to want a cooking pot that day. Alternatively, you would have to exchange your cooking pots for something the shoe-maker wanted. You could spend several days engaged in long chains of bartering before you eventually obtained your shoes.

We thus hit upon the idea of money. Instead of exchanging goods directly, we exchanged our goods for a common medium. This medium has changed from time to time, and from place to place. Salt was once a popular medium (hence the word 'salary'), as was gold. The more formal medium of coins and notes followed.

Today we don't even physically exchange these tokens much of the time – we wipe a piece of plastic through a piece of machinery to alter the configuration of some electron patterns in a computer many miles away. Yet we think money is real!

Take a look at, say, a £10 note. The wording on it reads: 'I promise to pay the bearer on demand the sum of ten pounds'. In other words, the piece of paper is *not* ten pounds, it is merely a promise by the Chief Cashier of the Bank of England to exchange the note for ten pounds. Originally, this meant you could turn up at the Bank of England and demand your £10's worth of gold. Today, the Bank of England won't exchange the note for anything other than another note or the equivalent value in coins! Not only is the £10 note not the real ten pounds, but we can't even exchange it for the real ten pounds! It's nothing but an idea.

We all have ideas. The difference between someone who makes money out of their ideas and someone who doesn't is that the people who make money *act* on their ideas.

The idea doesn't have to be spectacular. It doesn't have to be clever. It doesn't have to be complex. Pet Rocks, Hula-Hoops, Frisbees, Cabbage-Patch dolls ... countless fortune-making ideas are ridiculously simple. But it isn't true that the world will beat a path to your

Figure 9

Potential money-making ideas

Figure 9 Continued

door when you design a better mouse-trap: *you* have to be the one to decide to act.

Make a list in Figure 9 of all the potential money-making ideas you've had and not acted on. Keep adding to this list. And start viewing them as potential money-makers. Most of them may be no good. But another difference between those who make money from ideas and those who don't is this: those who do don't give up after one idea.

■ 9 ■

Inventing new rules

■ New rules for old.

In step 7, you clarified your existing relationship to money. These thoughts, beliefs, ideas and opinions are not reality. For every belief you have about money, someone out there has the opposite belief. As we said in step 1, we each *think* our version is reality, because life seems to bear us out. But this is no more than a self-fulfilling prophecy: because we think something is true, we act consistently with that belief. We invent rules based on our beliefs. We go looking for evidence, and find it. We don't even notice the times when something happens which contradicts our rules, or – if we do – we dismiss it as an exception, a fluke, a one-off.

For example, if you believe that money doesn't come easily, you will formulate a rule that the way to earn money is to work hard. You'll work hard, earn money and 'prove' the value of your rule and thus the truth of your belief.

But it is your rule that leads you to shy away from opportunities of making money effortlessly! Any such opportunities will seem either unreal or somehow wrong. You'll dismiss them out of hand, never make money from them and thus gather more evidence for your rule.

If this happens to be one of your rules, we're not picking on you! We *all* have rules about money, and we all gather evidence for them. None of us chose our rules. We learned them during childhood from our parents, our friends, TV, books ... all kinds of sources. Mainly we learn them from our parents/guardians; psychologists estimate that about 60 per cent of our fundamental attitudes to life are established by the time we are four years old. Try this:

If you could encapsulate into a single saying or sentence your father's philosophy regarding money, what would it be? This might be something he actually said often (for example, *Money doesn't grow on trees*) or it might just be a sentence that summarizes a whole range of different things he said. Write that sentence here:

_____

_____

Now do the same for your mother:

_____

_____

(If you were brought up by someone other than your parents, pick the two most significant people.)

Now do the same for yourself. This might be a little more difficult, because we are not aware of our philosophy *as a philosophy*. We think our philosophy is reality. A good way to think about it is to pick a friend or relative who knows you well, but has a different approach to money, and think about how they would describe your philo-sophy regarding money. Write that here:

_____

_____

Your philosophy is likely to be:

- One of the above.
- A combination of the two.
- The exact opposite of one of the above.
- The exact opposite of a combination of the two.

So, none of us had a choice about our philosophy or rules about money. And yours is no more valid than anyone else's. And yet our whole experience of money is determined by our rules. Given this, we think it makes sense to try out new rules. Rules which support us rather than undermining us.

Start by making a list of your existing rules on the left-hand page of Figure 10. And then examine each one in turn. Ask yourself whether the rule is a support or a hindrance. If it's a hindrance, pick a more supportive rule – the exact opposite is often suitable – and write it on the right-hand page of Figure 10.

Let's suppose you have a rule which says _Look after the pennies and the pounds will look after themselves._ As a result of this rule, you never spend money frivolously, not even very small amounts. Or, if you do, you feel guilty about it. You might choose a new rule which says _Enjoy the fruit of your work._

If you have a rule which says _Spend today, for tomorrow you die_, you might invent a new rule which says _A penny saved is a penny earned._

Note that we're not trying to persuade you to adopt any particular philosophy. All we want is for you to live by rules which support you and your aims in life. If an existing rule works well for you, keep it –

Old rules

Figure 10

New rules

Figure 10 Continued

don't change a thing. You only want to change a rule if it doesn't work ... if it makes you or your family miserable, or if it stops you living the life you want to live. And remember that this is a game. You can afford to try things out, see if they work, just as you might try a new grip in tennis. If the new rule doesn't work, go back to the old one, or try a new variation.

If you find yourself slipping into the trap of thinking your old philosophy is reality, do some research: test your old ideas against some facts. For example, you think that money is in short supply, that there isn't enough for everyone? *Fact*: there is the currency equivalent of more than five million billion US dollars in circulation. That's enough money for every man, woman and child on the planet to be a dollar millionaire. There is no shortage of money.

Once you've listed your old rules in the left-hand column of Figure 10, write your new ones in the right-hand column.

Now comes the tough bit: try living by these rules!

This will be difficult. You've lived by your old rules for a long time. You have ample evidence that they work. Intellectually, you may know them to be arbitrary, but emotionally you believe they are reality.

Start small. If you have a new rule which tells you to spend where the old one told you to save, treat yourself to a few small luxuries. They don't have to be especially expensive – a magazine, a box of chocolates, a bouquet of flowers, a paperback book, a trip to the theatre ... anything which you would not have done under the old rule.

Arm yourself with facts. Every time you start slipping into thinking the old rules are more real, do some research. Spend time with people who have the opposite rules to you. Read books written by people who have different rules. Listen out for people with different rules on the radio and television, on the street, at work, at parties. ...

This step requires commitment. It needs to be done consciously, each day. But it does work. Little by little, you'll accumulate new evidence. Through living by different rules, your experience of life will alter. Stick with it.

■ 10 ■

The source of all financial problems

■ What is the source of all financial problems?

Give the question some thought and write all the possible answers which come to mind into the box in Figure 11.

Now look over all your answers, and pick the one you think is *the source* of all the rest. Write that one here:

_____

The source of all financial problems

Figure 11

We suggest that the source of all financial problems is: *Wanting*.

(In fact, you could leave out the word 'financial' and the answer would be the same. There are other answers that amount to the same thing: comparison, contrast, focusing on what is not, and so on.)

If we didn't want anything, we would have no financial problems. Whatever we did and didn't have would be fine with us. No problems.

Unfortunately, while this is all well and good as an exercise in philosophy, it's not a particularly useful answer in practice. We're human, and we will always want things. We will always be aware of the contrast between what we have and what we want. But it does open the way to a question with a more useful answer:

■   What is the source of *your* financial problems?

It's wanting, for sure. But what is it you actually want? In step 1, we argued that it's not money, but rather the things you can do with the money. And in this step we go a stage further and argue that it's not even the things you can do with the money, it's *what you would be if you had/had done all those things.*

In other words, what you would have achieved if you owned all the possessions you listed in step 1, had done everything, lived the lifestyle, given away the money. . . .

Put in an even simpler form, *why do you want those things?*

Here's how we suggest you answer the question. Look through your list. Imagine that you have everything on your list. You have the houses, the cars, the boats, the planes, the horses, the clothes, the gadgets, the land, the businesses, the charitable foundations, the jetset lifestyle, the holidays . . . the lot.

Now, write down what that would have achieved for you. Who or what would you be if you had it all. What quality would sum up your life? Pick a word or phrase that describes the experience you would have. For example, the word might be 'successful'. Or 'free'. Or 'powerful'. Respected. Loved. Relaxed. Secure. Calm. Influential ... whatever the experience would be for you, if you had that life.

You may think of more than one word. That's fine. Write them all down in the left-hand column of Figure 12 and then – when you've done that – pick the one that is the most important, or incorporates the rest.

Write this word or phrase in the right-hand column. And be honest with yourself – the exercise is a waste of time if you're not.

We're now going to say something that's hard to hear. Your initial response may be to argue against it, or deny it. All we ask is that, when you've done that, you give it some thought. You may find that, on reflection, you agree. Here's the claim:

The quality you wrote in the right-hand box is the key quality that is presently missing from your life. You are not . . . [whatever you wrote in the box].

It's hard to hear because that quality is so important to you. You want that quality more than anything else.

Think about it. You would spend an incredible amount of money buying and doing everything on your list. And what would all that money, all those things, get you? The quality you wrote in the box. Clearly if you would devote all that money, time and energy to achieving that quality, the quality must be (*a*) missing and (*b*) crucially important to you. And since the source of all financial problems is wanting, and what you want more than anything else is that quality, the lack of that quality in your life is the source of all your financial problems.

We're not saying that, if you achieved that quality, you wouldn't need money. You would. Money is a practical tool. But, if you could achieve that quality in your life, money would not have the same power and hold over you that it has at present. You would be able to view it as a tool at your disposal, rather than being at its mercy. You would, in short, be able to see money as a game.

If I had everything on my list, then I would be . . .	The most important of these, or the umbrella term, is . . .

Figure 12

■ 11 ■

Resolving your financial problems

■ Money does not buy prosperity.

In step 10 we argued that the source of our financial problems has nothing to do with money, but is, rather, the lack of the key quality in our lives. You may have listed several qualities. But whatever term or terms you identified, there is an umbrella term that embraces all of them. A term which means the state of having it all, having nothing missing. That term is 'prosperity'.

We think prosperity involves having lots of money. We reason that money will enable us to buy all the things that would bring us the quality we seek. It won't. We've met multi-millionaires who still do not consider themselves successful, powerful, free, happy, loved, respected, influential or whatever their key quality happened to be. They may have a comfortable lifestyle. They may not lie awake at nights worrying about how to pay the bills. They may even have all the material possessions they want. But it doesn't give them the quality they seek. They are not prosperous. And all the money in the world couldn't make them prosperous. Because prosperity is not a function of money.

Don't misunderstand us. We like money. Some money is necessary, more is pleasant. But it is not a route to prosperity.

Money as a route to prosperity is a confidence trick, and we are all victims of that con. We want to be prosperous. We think that more money will make us prosperous. We devote large chunks of our lives to making money in order to become prosperous. We work hard, start businesses, invest money, save money ... and then discover that, even when we have more money, we're still not prosperous. So we think we need still more money, so we make even more money and we're *still* not prosperous. But we keep trying, believing that eventually we'll have enough money to feel prosperous.

It never happens. Not when we make a million, not if we made a billion. Millionaires and billionaires don't feel any more prosperous than anyone else. They have the lifestyle, the possessions, the trappings, but go talk to a few: they do not feel prosperous.

It's a confidence trick, and the con is this: we believe we are not prosperous. That's the trick. Babies are born prosperous. For them, nothing is missing. They have what they have, don't have what they don't have, and they are who they are. They live in the present. They don't worry about the future. Happiness is a full belly and some attention. They don't tell themselves that they will be happy when they've got a better dummy, a bigger pram and more money in their piggy bank than the baby next door. Babies are prosperous, right now, with nothing missing and nothing to achieve.

But very early on we start to decide that something is missing. We soon want that bigger and better toy. Right through into adulthood when we want to earn more, make more, have more. . . . We are then part of the confidence game of trying to become prosperous. It's a con because *we already are*. We were born prosperous. We didn't lose our prosperity with our milk teeth. It's still there, we just don't experience it. The only difference between us and a baby is that the baby doesn't have a 'little voice' inside its head telling it that things should be different.

We spend our lives trying to become prosperous. We work for it,

strive for it, become driven or anxious or stressed or resigned. . . .
Every now and then we achieve something that leaves us feeling
more prosperous. A pay rise, a new house, a new car, better furniture,
a more sophisticated hifi, more gadgets, designer clothes. . . . But the
effect wears off. Soon we find that we don't feel any more prosperous
than we did before. So we set our sights on the next thing, the next
step, the next level, thinking that will make us prosperous. And so on.

It's all a con.

But what difference does it make, knowing it's a con? We still need
money, we still want the house, the car, the furniture, hifi, gadgets,
clothes. . . .

This is the difference: people who know it's a con aren't making
money and buying things *in order to* become prosperous. We still do
the same things. We still make money, spend it, invest it, save it. But
we're doing it *as a game*, and we do so because money is the best game
in town. It's the game that the world is playing. We could opt out –
refuse to play – but we play because it's fun. And the aim of the game
is to make money. That's why part of this book is dedicated to
making more money: not because more money is better, not because
you'll be more prosperous if you have more money, but simply
because that's the aim of the game.

Prosperity is experiencing yourself as prosperous, right now, irrespective of your financial state. Prosperity is seeing the con for what it is
so that you can then play the money game *as a game*. Not for dear life.

If you're currently broke, you have a huge advantage over those who
have plenty of money. Because, when you have plenty of money,
and feel prosperous, you may believe that your prosperity is a result
of the money. When you're broke, and feel prosperous, you know
it's not the money. And this book isn't about having more or less
money, except as a game – it's about living a prosperous life, a life in
which you experience your own prosperity.

How can we experience prosperity as distinct from money? There
are three steps:

- Acknowledge that your key quality is currently missing (most of us start by denying it).
- Actively seek it out in yourself and those around you (we want it so much it's hard to see it in others).
- Acknowledge the quality when you see it.

For example, if your key quality is 'freedom', start by acknowledging the fact that you don't experience or express freedom. Just admit that to yourself.

Next, look for it. Seek it out. When you act freely in a way you normally don't, notice that. When friends, family, colleagues, strangers, act freely, notice that. Actively look for evidence of freedom around you. If you see plenty of evidence of the *lack* of the quality, seek out exceptions, counter-examples, alternative interpretations.

Finally, acknowledge the quality in other people. Comment on it. Congratulate them on it. Make this a habit for at least a fortnight. This step may be hard. We don't like the fact that the quality is missing in our own life, and it's the one quality we want more than any other, so it can be distressing to acknowledge the fact that others possess that quality. But remember: it's a con. You are, in fact, free, successful, powerful, respected, loved, relaxed, secure, calm, influential . . . whatever your key quality, you already possess it. You simply don't experience it at the moment. And acknowledging it in others is one of the most effective ways of experiencing it in your own life.

None of this is a guarantee that you will always feel prosperous, all of the time. Nor that you won't want more money, and the things money can buy. You will. But the key point is to distinguish prosperity from money. As long as you are clear that more money doesn't lead to prosperity, you are free of the con, and free to play with money as a game.

◼ 12 ◼

Get your money back

◼ Have someone else pay for this book.

The last couple of steps have been tough, so it's time for a break. Here's a simple assignment: generate *at least* the price you paid for this book from an unexpected source.

The amount you generate can be exactly the cost of the book, or many times more. It can be cash, goods or services. You can do it in any legal and ethical way you choose. The only condition is that it has to be money or value you would not otherwise have received.

Ask for a pay rise or bonus. If you run your own business, put up your prices a little. Negotiate a special discount on something you're buying. Negotiate a freebie, or an upgrade, of some kind. Anything you like. But complete this step before going any further, and in any case within 48 hours.

We all have ways of creating additional money when we really need it, but we tend to take advantage of this ability only in emergencies. We recommend making a habit of it. Make a list of all the ways you could generate additional money or value. Small ways and big ways

Ways of generating extra money or value

Figure 13

alike. Add to this list at least once a week. And use it for pleasure as well as coping with crises.

And, if you fancy a challenge, try for the record! At the time of writing, the record from this step during The Money Course was a man who negotiated a deal which netted him $2.3 million. He had been working on the project for a year, and abandoned it three months before he took The Money Course; after the course, he sold the project as an idea. . . .

■ 13 ■

Pluck money out of the air!

■ Sell some ideas

Step 8 argued that all money comes from ideas. Usually, we turn the ideas into some kind of product or service before we sell it. But even that isn't always necessary: we can sells ideas themselves!

Try this. Think of an idea (or use the one below). It doesn't have to be anything spectacular or dramatic – it needn't change the world – just something that other people might find useful or fun or both.

Go and offer to sell someone an idea. The deal is as follows. You'll tell them the idea, and the price, in advance. They are then free to buy it or not as they please. If they want to use it, however, they have to buy it. So their two options are to decline the idea, in which case they don't pay for it and can't use it, or to buy it, in which case they are free to use it *and* to sell it to someone else.

Make at least ten sales for at least £1 each. You can sell ten different ideas, or the same one ten times to ten different people, and you can charge as much as you like, but you must make at least ten sales and charge at least £1 each time.

If you hate the idea of selling, and the thought of selling ideas makes you cringe, this step will be ten times more powerful for you than for someone who is happy about selling; you should make 20 sales!

Here's an idea you're free to sell. It's called Jackpot Tipping.

> Ever wished you could afford to leave a waiter or waitress a massive tip when you receive absolutely perfect service? With this idea, you can.
>
> Whenever you eat out, notice how the standard of service compares to your idea of perfect service. Then leave a tip in direct proportion to the standard of service. For example, if the service was half as good as your ideal, leave half your usual tip. If it was 80 per cent perfect, leave 80 per cent of your usual tip. If it didn't even get on the scale, leave nothing. And so on.
>
> Every time you do this, put the balance of the tip aside. Stick it in a savings account or keep it in a cashbox at home or something. Let's take an example. The meal cost £40, and you would normally leave a 12.5 per cent tip. Your normal tip would thus be £5. The service was 75 per cent perfect, so you leave 75 per cent of £5 as a tip (£3.75) and put the balance (£1.25) aside. Keep a running tally in your wallet, but always physically put the money aside.
>
> Do this every time you eat out. Then, when the day finally arrives that you receive absolutely 100 per cent perfect service ... when the waiter/waitress gave a warm welcoming smile, offered you a choice of table, answered all your questions about the menu fully and cheerfully, took your order promptly, delivered the meal unobtrusively, never bothered you but was always available when you wanted something, removed your plates when they were empty, topped up your wine – the works ... when that day comes, you check your wallet tally to see how much you have set aside over the days, weeks, months or even years it has taken to receive perfect service. This is the jackpot tip, and your perfect waiter or waitress has just won it.

Invite them over. Ask them to pull up a chair and sit down. Explain what you have been doing, and that they have offered you perfect service, and then present them with their jackpot tip! (If the amount is substantial, you may need to arrange with the restaurant to include the tip in the credit card total for payment to the waiter/waitress.)

We know some people who have built up a jackpot many times greater than the value of the meal, hundreds of pounds in some cases. And the beauty of it is that it hasn't cost you a penny more than you would have spent had you just left everyone your standard tip.

Jackpot tipping is a great game. People who win big jackpot tips never forget it. It's something they will tell their grandchildren. And it will affect the way you view yourself and money: suddenly you have become someone who can afford to leave a bigger tip than the cost of the meal. And – as a bonus – you'll receive the full VIP treatment whenever you eat there in future!

■ 14 ■

Give away money . . .

■ Break the iron grip of scarcity.

Step 9 invited you to make up some new rules, and develop some new habits as a result. Here's a habit we particularly recommend: giving away money.

Most of us have a rule or idea that money is scarce, that we need to hang onto, or build up, whatever amount we have. This leads us to experience the world in a particular way, confirming our rule. The most effective way to break the iron grip of the scarcity rule is to give away money.

You probably think you can't afford to give away money. It's not true. Write down, in the space provided, exactly how much money you have right now, in your bank and savings accounts, in your wallet or purse, in your pockets, in your car – everywhere you have cash. Write down the exact total amount you think you have:

£_____ . ____

Now check it. If you got the amount precisely right, to the penny, you might convince us that you need every last penny. Otherwise, you have some money you'll never miss, even if it's just a few pounds or even a few pence.

Start giving away money, every day, for at least a week. Give it away in ways you wouldn't have done before. It needn't be much, but give just a little bit more than feels completely comfortable, otherwise you're still operating from your old rule.

Have fun with this step! You may have come across a phrase that has been appearing in graffiti in many large cities: *Commit random acts of kindness and senseless acts of beauty.* This has almost become a movement in some areas. On San Francisco's Golden Gate bridge, someone paid two toll fees: once for their own car, and again for the unknown car behind them. 'Tell them it's a gift from me', said the driver as he drove off with a grin. This has now become a tradition: when you cross the bridge, your toll is paid; you're paying for the car behind you.

Surya once got held up at a ticket machine when he was in a hurry to catch a train. A woman in front of him was slowly buying a ticket by shoving in an endless supply of small coins, with pauses while she searched her purse for the next few. Surya was growing more and more frustrated by the delay, until he realized that he didn't have to wait. He reached over, put in the rest of her fare, handed her the ticket with a grin, bought his own ticket and ran for his train while the woman stared open-mouthed after him.

There are endless opportunities. Next time you see a car in danger of being clamped or towed because the meter has expired, shove in a coin to buy some more time. Ever been stuck behind someone at a checkout when they realize they don't have quite enough money? Pay the difference for them. Someone stops you and asks you to change a coin? Give them the change but refuse their coin! People will think you're nuts – it's great fun.

Become equally adept at receiving gifts gracefully. People love to give, and very few of us are good at receiving. When a friend makes a (genuine) offer to pay for a meal, accept and thank them rather than arguing. Someone told a story of the best response they'd ever had to a gift: they bought a friend a watch; when he received it, the friend pulled off his old watch, put on the new one, and threw the old one in the bin.

■ 15 ■

Track all income and expenses to the penny

■ Take control of your finances.

You know those times when you open your wallet or purse and ask yourself what happened to the money you put in there just the other day? This is your chance to find out.

Most of us have no idea where our money goes. Especially cash. It comes in and goes out almost of its own accord. We are not in control of our finances. And if we aren't in control of our finances, how can we hope to achieve our income and net worth goals?

The first step towards control is awareness. Before you can control your finances, you need to become aware of them. That's the purpose of this step.

The assignment is to track all income and expenses, to the penny, for one week. Every penny you receive, every penny you spend, will be logged on the form in Figure 14 (just copy as many forms as you need).

It sounds like a chore, but it can be a revelation. Most people are

Income for week beginning:	Sheet ____ of ____	
Source	Amount	
Total carried forward to next sheet		

Figure 14

Expenses for week beginning:	Sheet ____ of ____	
Item	Amount	
Total carried forward to next sheet		

Figure 14 Continued

amazed at what they discover. Almost everyone finds that they spend money in ways they never imagined. Many people find they are spending money in ways they would never choose had they realized the true cost. (It is well-known, for example, that most smokers have little idea of the cost of their habit. Someone who smokes 20 cigarettes a day, of an average brand, is spending about £1000 a year at the time of writing.) Yet others find the opposite: a treat they really enjoy but indulge only occasionally costs next to nothing, and could easily be budgeted for as a regular purchase.

Once you become aware of your spending patterns, you are in a position to change them if you wish. With accurate information at your fingertips, you are able to manage your finances in such a way that you choose your lifestyle, rather than having it determined by habit or circumstance. (This is a point we'll expand on later in the book.)

Begin tracking all income and expenses for one week, starting now.

■ 16 ■

Treat yourself

■ Be purposefully extravagant.

Another way of changing your experience of money is to spend money in ways you normally wouldn't consider. Treat yourself, or treat someone else, but spend money in a way that gives you pleasure, and in a way you normally think extravagant.

Again, you don't need large sums of money to be able to do this. A treat can be as small as a chocolate bar, a magazine, a paperback book. Anything you normally would consider an extravagance. Conversely, if you have plenty of money to spend, buy something spectacular.

The amount doesn't matter, just the fact that you are spending money in a way you wouldn't when living by your old rules. Take a taxi when you would normally take a bus. Fly business class instead of economy, or first class instead of business class. Buy yourself a bouquet of flowers. When eating out, pick a restaurant in a higher price bracket than your normal choice. Buy a book in hardback rather than waiting for the paperback. Go away for the weekend. Have a shoe-shine. Hire a bigger car. Buy the more expensive brand of soap. Take a flying lesson. Buy two magazines instead of one. Hire a professional gardener to blitz the garden. Anything. Just make it something you consider extravagant.

Treat yourself, or someone else, extravagantly at least once a week. (But if you normally treat yourself and not others, treat someone else; if you normally treat others and not yourself, treat yourself.)

■ 17 ■

Create a
'Hot 100' list

■ What do you want?

Create a 'wish-list' of 100 items or services you wish you had and don't now have. It doesn't matter what they cost; they can cost a pound or two or a hundred million pounds. Include the trivial as well as the important, but only those things you don't already buy (you could, however, list a more expensive item where you already own a cheaper version). Against each one, put the approxiimate cost.

This is a *personal* list. Couples should each construct separate lists. As with the money genie exercise, include only what you actually want — not what you might one day want. The difference between this and step 1 is that, in step 1, you were assuming that you had a large sum of money to spend. In this step, you are assuming nothing. You are not setting out to spend a sum of money. You are listing things you really do want in your life today.

Do this now, utilizing Figure 15 and taking as much time as you like.

Now look through your list. Most people find that their list is a curious mixture of the wildly expensive and the surprisingly cheap.

Item	Cost	Item	Cost

Figure 15

Item	Cost	Item	Cost

Figure 15 Continued

In fact, you may well have listed items you could afford today, if you made that item a priority and allocated a budget to it.

Even if something looks unattainable, it ain't necessarily so. Not a few Rolls-Royce owners are people with very ordinary incomes – they are simply so passionate about the car that they've saved for years and remortgaged the house to buy it. They hire it out for weddings to pay for its upkeep.

Take each item in turn and ask yourself whether you are determined to have it, or would merely like it. Highlight or underline the ones you are determined to get. There seems to be a curious phenomenon at work once you decide you're going to do or get something. The climber William Murray observed that 'the moment one definitely commits oneself, then providence moves too. All sorts of things occur to help one that would never otherwise have occurred.'

Start acting consistently with your commitment. If something could be within your reach if you budgeted and/or saved for it, do that. Take every opportunity open to you. If you want a car, enter every competition with a car as the prize; you'd be amazed how few people enter most competitions – the odds are often much better than you realize.

Ask yourself whether you actually need to buy everything on your list. For example, if you want a speedboat, but would actually only use it a few times a year, find out if hiring one would be a viable option. Do you really want a chauffeur-driven limousine, or do you simply want the experience of arriving somewhere in one? They're available for hire by the hour. And so on.

For now, pick the one item on your list that you want more than all the rest, find out the exact cost and start looking at what it would take to have it . . . including the need to make more money.

■ 18 ■

Multiply your value ten-fold

■ Create your own circumstances.

Imagine that you are being paid ten times your current salary or fee. How would you do things differently? How would you perform the work? How would you present yourself? How would you behave in meetings? How would you handle enquiries? Ask yourself how you would perform each part of your working day if you were being paid ten times as much.

Now start doing this! Pretend you are being paid ten times as much, and perform your work accordingly. Aim to deliver ten times as much value, give ten times more service.

Most people are waiting to be paid more, *then* they'll deliver greater value, *then* they'll be of greater service. It works either way round, but one way leaves you waiting for the right circumstances to occur, the other gives you the power to create the circumstances you want.

This does not, of course, mean that if you start putting ten times as much into your work your boss or clients will suddenly turn round and offer you ten times as much money. But consider this.

Fees and salaries are determined by ourselves to a far greater extent than most of us appreciate. We don't apply for a particular job because the salary is outside the range we think we can earn. We limit our fees to a certain range because we think that's the amount clients will pay. Very often we never even consider jobs or assignments above a certain financial ceiling. It's not that we try and fail to achieve such income levels: we don't make the attempt in the first place. The problem is not an inability to convince others of our worth, the problem is an inability to convince *ourselves*.

This perceived income ceiling becomes a self-fulfilling prophecy. We apply for a certain level of jobs and contracts because – consciously or unconsciously – that's what we consider ourselves to be worth. Our CV or project portfolio is thus one of a consistent range of work, which makes it difficult to apply for higher-paying work.

Acting as if you are paid ten times as much is a method of changing your self-perception. Done wholeheartedly, it can be almost miraculously effective. We know many people who have achieved huge leaps in salary or fee-level through this approach.

There are no guarantees. There are many factors which affect the salary or fee you are able to command, ranging from your competence at the job to worldwide economic conditions. Some factors you can control, others you can't. But this is one you can, and it's perhaps the most important of all because it's the one which determines the level at which you will *attempt* to succeed.

Don't limit this approach to your work. Put ten times as much into *all* aspects of your life. Your relationships, your social life, your hobbies ... everything. It sounds exhausting, but – curiously – it seems to be a case of the more you give, the more you have available to give. Anyone who plays an active sport will know this phenomenon. You may feel tired and lethargic before the game, but if you throw yourself in wholeheartedly, giving your all, you soon find hidden reserves of energy. And the harder you play, the more energy you find.

Aim to deliver ten times as much value, be of ten times more service, in all aspects of your life. Being of service to, and generating value for, others is one of the main keys to prosperity.

■ 19 ■

Prepare to manage wealth

■ In one easy step.

A simple step. Open one additional current account, and three savings accounts, preferably with the bank which holds your main personal current account. We'll explain their purpose later in the book, but we want you to have them open, ready for when they are needed. All we'll say now is that these accounts are the basis for having money available for the key aspects of your life, no matter what your current level of income . . .

■ 20 ■

Changing reality

■ Reality is not fixed.

Language determines the way in which we experience the world. Indeed, some philosophers go further than this and argue that language literally *creates* reality. Either way, altering the language we use will change our experience of reality.

Propaganda experts are well aware of the role of language in defining experience. A bombing mission resulting in 'collateral damage' sounds a lot more acceptable than a mission which killed innocent civilians. Advertisers know that 'crisp, golden, wholewheat biscuits baked to perfection and then generously coated in a luxurious layer of smooth, creamy milk chocolate' sounds much more appealing than 'chocolate biscuits'. And market traders know that '£9.99' is a more attractive price than '£10' (none of us imagine we're fooled by it, but it continues to work just the same).

We therefore propose alternative terms for three of the four key ways in which we relate to money, terms which are designed to provide us with a more empowering view. Try on the new terms for size. Where we offer more than one alternative term, use whichever you prefer.

For earning, we suggest *creating* or *generating*. Earning implies that we have to do something in order to justify receiving the money. It suggests that we have to work for the money. More than this, it suggests that our income will be directly proportional to the effort we put into generating it, that creating more money requires harder work. The most cursory glance at the world around us shows this to be nonsense, but most of us still believe it.

The myth is occasionally reinforced by tales of millionaires who built up a successful business from nothing by working sixteen hours a day, a lifestyle they continue to this day. A brief survey of millionaires will quickly demonstrate that such people are the exceptions rather than the rule.

Using the term 'creating' or 'generating' implies merely that we are in some way responsible for producing the money, not that it will require work or effort.

For saving, we suggest *accumulating* or *collecting* or *gathering*. Saving suggests sacrifice over long periods of time, and has connotations of scrooge-like behaviour: the idea that accumulating money is an alternative to spending it, rather than complementary to it. Again, most people who are successful at accumulating money also have plenty available to spend.

The terms 'accumulating', 'collecting' and 'gathering' all imply an easy accumulation of surplus funds, rather than miserly behaviour.

For spending, we suggest *giving* or *exchanging*. Spending implies that the money is literally 'spent' (used up, exhausted) at the end of the transaction. This is nonsense, since the money will be used again by the person receiving it: the money has as much value after the transaction as it did beforehand. Even considered from our own viewpoint, we haven't exhausted or used up the money, merely converted it into another form – a form we consider more useful or valuable than the original, otherwise we wouldn't have made the transaction.

Spending also has connotations for many of reluctance, a need for care and caution, something to be done only when necessary.

The term 'giving' or 'exchanging' is a more accurate reflection of the transaction, and implies freedom, willingness and plenty.

The fourth key way of relating to money is investing. We think this term works, but suggest *appreciating* as an alternative if investing has unwanted connotations for you.

All we're asking is for you to try on these terms for size, to see whether or not they have any impact on the way in which you relate to money, and – if so – whether that impact is a help or a hindrance. The purpose of suggesting alternative names is to empower you, so use whichever terms best achieve this.

■ 21 ■

Keeping your eye on the ball

■ Don't be stopped.

One of the basic laws of physics states that, for every action, there is an equal and opposite reaction. This fundamental law seems equally applicable in the world of emotion and thought. Every time we set a goal, we immediately (or soon afterwards) think of an equal number of reasons why we can't, or shouldn't, reach the goal. We see the potential flaws, we have doubts, guilt, cynicism, worries, memories of past failures ... to the point where we often succeed in talking ourselves out of even attempting the goal.

This is never more true than in the field of money. Most people are waiting for the one Great Idea, the one that doesn't bring all these negatives to mind. Then they'll know they have the right goal, the one worth working for, the one for which they'll give their all.

This will never happen.

The fears, doubts and uncertainties are an equal and opposite reaction to the goal. They are a *function* of the goal. Creating the goal creates the reasons we think it won't work, or shouldn't work.

Fears, uncertainties and doubts re: net worth and income goals

Figure 16

Creating a small goal creates small objections. Creating a large goal creates large objections. Equal and opposite.

The only difference between someone who follows through on their goals, pursuing them wholeheartedly, and someone who gives up before they've started is that the people who keep going, keep going. They experience the same fears, uncertainties and doubts as anyone else. They can see all the potential flaws as well as anyone else. But they keep their eye on the ball, and keep going regardless.

That's what it will take to achieve your financial goals. Go back to the financial goals you set in steps 4 and 5. We'll make two predictions:

- First, your goals probably already look silly to you. You already want to change them, or forget about them.
- Second, you can list plenty of reasons why it is impractical or immoral to achieve these goals.

List these reasons in Figure 16. Don't stop until you have listed every fear, uncertainty and doubt. Every reason why you should not attempt the goal. Every reason why you cannot succeed. Every last objection. If you need more space, continue on a separate sheet, but keep going until you've listed the lot:

(If you think of anything else later, go back and add it.)

The more ambitious your goals, the more objections you will have, and/or the more convincing those objections will seem.

Don't believe the objections.

We're not asking you to dismiss them out of hand, to ignore them or suppress them. Many of them will contain useful information which will help you in your project. But don't allow them to stop you. Don't assign any greater significance to them than you assigned to the original goals. Treat them as opinions.

Which leads us to the next step.

■ 22 ■

Commit yourself to your goals

■ Give one hundred per cent.

Interview a hundred self-made millionaires and you'll discover a hundred different 'secrets to success'. But there is one thing you'll find almost all of them have in common: they set themselves a goal, and then went after it, come hell or high water.

The same is true of people who consistently achieve success in any field, not just that of making money. They decide something is going to happen, and then go out and make it happen, no matter what.

Most people don't do this. They set half-hearted goals, pursue them in a half-hearted fashion, allow obstacles and opposition to deter them, and then wonder why they achieve half-hearted results.

You may not know how to achieve your goals. Most millionaires didn't know what they were doing when they started, but they were willing to find out how to do it along the way. They were willing to make mistakes. Willing to be laughed at. Willing to fail and keep going. The average self-made multi-millionaire has been bankrupt 2.8 times. Bankruptcy didn't stop them: they kept going.

Step 1: _____%

Step 2: _____%

Step 3: _____%

Step 4: _____%

Step 5: _____%

Step 6: _____%

Step 7: _____%

Step 8: _____%

Step 9: _____%

Step 10: _____%

Step 11: _____%

Step 12: _____%

Step 13: _____%

Step 14: _____%

Step 15: _____%

Step 16: _____%

Step 17: _____%

Step 18: _____%

Step 19: _____%

Step 20: _____%

Step 21: _____%

Add up the total: _____%

Now divide by 21 to get an average: _____%

Figure 17

A question: if we gave you a written guarantee that completing every step in this book, and doing each to the very best of your ability, would result in you achieving your financial goals within two years, would you do every step 100 per cent? If you don't complete each step 100 per cent, you'll never know.

We know that the system presented in this book produces results, often dramatic ones. We know that the system works *if people do it*. We have no idea whether doing some of the system half-heartedly produces results.

This step is halfway through the book. You can use this fact to assess your own level of commitment to the goals you set in steps 3 and 4. Look back at the first 21 steps of the book, and in Figure 17 give yourself an *honest* rating, from 1 to 100, in terms of how you approached each action step. A rating of 100 means that you completed the step in full, and gave it everything. A rating of zero means that you either skipped the step or didn't even begin the required activity.

We suggest that the average percentage, provided you completed the exercise honestly, is a good measure of your commitment to your income goals.

We invite you to choose a new level of commitment to steps 23 on, as well as going back and redoing any earlier steps where you feel you sold yourself short.

■ 23 ■

The secret of creating money

■ The only 'secret to success'.

There is a simple key to creating or generating money. That key is, in fact, the *only* way of turning an idea into cash.

It is more fundamental than any strategy or approach. It is what gives something value. It is what enables one person to earn a hundred times more than another. It is what makes one painting worth millions and another worth only a few pounds.

It is the one key thing which anyone must generate in order to generate money.

If there is any 'secret of success', this is it.

Agreement.

Value is not an objective entity. Value is not inherent in the universe, or ordained by God. Value exists only where people agree that it exists.

Two paintings may be in every respect identical to the naked eye, yet one is a Van Gogh and the other a clever forgery. There is, objectively, little to choose between them, yet one is worth millions and the other just a few thousand (one of the ironies of the art forgery business is that there is now a collector's market in known forgeries by certain artists). It is simply that art collectors consider – agree – that original masterpieces are valuable, and forgeries much less so.

The term 'masterpiece' is itself defined by agreement. Van Gogh's paintings were worth little when he was alive, regarded merely as amusing. Now they are considered some of the finest paintings in the world. The paintings are the same; the consensus of opinion has changed.

The key to creating money, therefore, is to generate agreement for the value of what you have to offer.

We all create agreement about who we are and what we have to offer. We generate this agreement by what we do, how we present ourselves, how we behave, how we dress, our appearance, our accent, our car, education, confidence and so on. We generate both wanted and unwanted agreement. The amount of money we now have is a function of the agreement we have generated to date. If we have only a little money, the agreement we have generated is that we have little financial value to offer; if we have accrued substantial wealth, the agreement we have generated is that we have a great deal of financial value to offer. Neither implies anything about our worth as a human being; it is simply useful information about the agreement we generate (another way of saying this would be the reputation we have) in terms of financial value.

Many books have been written on ways of increasing agreement for your success, from marketing schemes and business plans to power dressing and voice training. Some of these books are extremely useful. But the key to creating money in your own life is to examine the agreement *you* generate.

To do this, you need the services of one or more good friends — friends who will be honest with you.

Sit down with them, and ask them to tell you – honestly – what they think most people would say about you. The focus of this book is on money, so you will want to look particularly at the type of questions listed below, but you can make this step as broad as you wish, asking about the impression you give – the agreement you generate – in as many areas as you like.

Ask your friend what most people would say about your . . .

■   Income.
■   Competence.
■   Confidence.
■   Dress.
■   Speech.
■   Telephone manner.
■   Writing style.

And so on. The factors you choose will depend on your status (employed or self-employed) and occupation. If you are self-employed, or run your own business, ask also what most people would say about your . . .

■   Business card.
■   Letterhead.
■   Leaflet or brochure.
■   Telephone answering.
■   Testimonials.
■   Presentation style.
■   Sales letters.

And so on.

Action	Target date

Figure 18

Action	Target date

Figure 18 Continued

The answers are the agreement you generate at present. Some of the answers may be uncomfortable for you, and you may want to argue about them; don't. Check them by asking other friends, but don't prompt them.

Once you have answers to these questions, ask both yourself and your friend(s) what you could do to generate the best possible agreement for yourself as an employee or as a business. Anything which generates agreement for low value/low cost needs to be changed to something which generates agreement for high value/high cost.

Again, we're using money as our focus, but the same principle applies to other areas of life. For example, campaign groups need to generate agreement for their ideas. Environmentalists are a good example. Ten years ago, the agreement they generated was that they were cranks or, at least, rather intense, over-anxious types. Today, they generate agreement for themselves as thoughtful, responsible people with a message that needs to be heeded.

Produce a list of action steps required to change the agreement you generate. Some of these steps may be expensive (new suits, for example) and have to be achieved over time, while others may be both inexpensive and simple to achieve.

List your action plan in Figure 18 and schedule these actions in your diary, and tick them off as you complete each one.

■ 24 ■

Don't work for a living!

■ Do what you love.

While it may not be true that nobody ever got rich working for somebody else (quite a few people have achieved fairly comfortable lifestyles doing this), it is certainly true that few people get rich doing something they don't enjoy. And even if you manage to make money doing something you dislike, it is unlikely to promote a sense of prosperity.

We spend more of our waking life working than doing anything else. Yet millions of people perform work they hate 'to make a living'. They do this because 'earning a living' is their goal: they have no more ambitious goal to spur them into anything else.

Performing work which gives you no pleasure or satisfaction, for which you have no passion, is like death by hunger in developing countries, or homelessness in almost any country: we accept it not because it is acceptable, but because it is commonplace.

Yet it isn't necessary. People make money ('earn their living' and more) from all sorts of unlikely things. Racing cars. Flying

Things I love to do, and ways of making money from same

Figure 19

Things I love to do, and ways of making money from same

Figure 19 Continued

helicopters. Rock climbing (instructors and guides). Sleeping (sleep research subjects). Reading (for publishers). Eating (tasters and critics). Watching TV (critics). Travelling (travel writers, airline crews, couriers and so on). Walking dogs ... there is virtually no human activity at which it is impossible to earn a living.

We use the word 'impossible' advisedly. We do not claim that switching careers to something you love will necessarily be easy. We're not advocating that you hand in your resignation tomorrow morning and blithely assume that you will wander happily into your new career the day after. Switching career often takes time and work. But if you're doing so to spend the bulk of your life engaged in an activity you love, isn't it worth the effort?

If you're planning to make a lot of money, we recommend doing it through an activity about which you are passionate.

Make a list in Figure 19 of all the things you love to do, and then 'brainstorm' ways of making money out of them (by 'brainstorm', we mean write down any and all the ideas that occur to you, no matter how ridiculous or far-fetched). Choose one that appeals to you. And begin creating a plan of action for turning a fun idea into a career you love.

■ 25 ■

Learn lessons
from money

■ Predict the unpredictable.

One of the difficulties of taking control of our finances is that the practice rarely seems to follow the theory. There are always unexpected expenses – seemingly random events that defy our budgets and forecasts.

But it is often possible to predict the unpredictable. When an unexpected expense arises, for example, notice how it was that the expense wasn't expected. Is it something which, while not specifically predictable, is likely to turn up from time to time? If you keep records of your bills, look back through them for other unexpected bills; are there any discernible patterns, or at least a typical total amount in such bills each year?

For example, nobody can predict that their car's fuel pump is going to fail on 15 June, but it is possible to estimate an annual amount for unscheduled car repairs. You can't predict that a storm will blow some tiles off your roof, but you can estimate an annual amount for house repairs. You can't foresee dropping a personal stereo or leaving your coat on a train, but – again – you can estimate the likely

Date	Item	Cost

Figure 20

annual cost of such mishaps. And you can include these estimated amounts in your monthly budget.

Look through your financial records and list unexpected items in Figure 20.

Look for patterns, or at least an average monthly amount. Include an Unexpected Expenses item in your budget equivalent to this amount.

If you *don't* keep records of your bills, consider doing so. The intention is to create a relationship with money in which you are in control, and a prerequisite of control is accurate information.

Similarly when you *receive* unexpected money, goods or services: could you do it again, deliberately? Even if the item is not totally within your control, are there steps you can take to make such occurrences more likely? The same applies when you save money: could you do so on a regular basis?

Again, make a list in Figure 21 of all the unexpected receipts and savings you can recall or look up in your records, and see which are repeatable.

Not everything is repeatable, of course. If you win a holiday in a competition, you cannot take any action to repeat this beyond entering future competitions. But even with seemingly chance events, you can take steps to maximize your chances. If you enjoy competitions, for example, there are several magazines that tell you which competitions are on offer and where, and give you a panel's opinion on the answers to the competition questions. Most such magazines guarantee to refund your money if you don't win more in prizes than the subscription cost. Many competitions attract remarkably few entries, giving each competitor a significant chance.

Finally, there is one lesson we recommend you learn from other people's experience: never lend money to friends and family – make it a gift instead. More relationships are damaged by money than any other single cause. Call the money a loan if it makes the recipient

Date	Item	Amount

Figure 21

happier, and allow them to pay the same amount to you later, but always view it as a gift yourself. That way it won't affect the relationship whether or not they repay.

■ 26 ■

Have a purpose for creating money

■ Give yourself direction.

You have already created financial goals. But goals in themselves are rather dry and sterile, and unlikely to see you through obstacles and setbacks. You also need a *purpose* for creating money.

A purpose is at a higher logical level than a goal. It is the reason you set your goals. A purpose reflects your values and attitudes; the goals exist to serve your purpose.

For example, some possible purposes for creating money might be:

- To be, do and have anything you choose.
- To provide the very best for your family.
- To fully support the cause(s) you love.

Unlike a goal, a purpose is ongoing. It is not something to be achieved and then left behind, but something which gives your life direction; something which will motivate you in good times and tough times alike. And it is completely subjective: all that matters is that it works for you. It doesn't even have to make sense to anyone else.

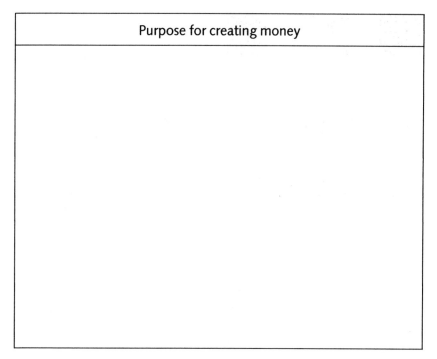

Figure 22

Choose a purpose for creating money, and write it in the box in Figure 22.

■ 27 ■

The secret of successful saving

■ Saving made easy.

Saving seems to divide the world into two types of people: those who save as easily as they breathe, and those for whom saving is an alien concept.

The ability or inability to save has nothing to do with disposable income: many people with tiny disposable incomes manage to save very successfully, while others with plenty of money to play with never seem to accumulate a penny.

Here's the secret...

The secret of successful saving is to put aside a regular amount, every week or every month, without fail, and to leave the money alone until you've saved enough.

To natural savers, that is so obvious as to sound absurd. To those who have never succeeded in saving, it is a revelation. Unsuccessful savers either don't save regularly, they just put a bit aside now and then when they have some spare cash, and/or they frequently 'borrow' from their savings intending to replace the cash later. They thus never accumulate the money in the first place, or spend it as soon as it reaches any significant amount.

It doesn't matter how little you can afford to save: if you set aside a fixed amount each week or month, and leave it in the account, you will accumulate money. Even a pound a month gets you into the saving habit, and has your accounts up and running.

■ 28 ■

Set up a Master Cashflow account

■ For automatic financial management.

This step will enable you to track all your income and expenses to the penny, with minimal effort on your part, and to ensure that the key aspects of your life are all regularly and automatically funded.

Rename your main personal current account your Master Cashflow account (you may like to ask your bank to rename the account as your name followed by 'Master Cashflow account' so that this name will appear on the account paperwork). This account will act as a clearing house for all your income and outgoings.

All income is paid into this account, before being transferred to other accounts as detailed in the next few steps, and *all* outgoings are paid through this account.

Use Figure 23 to track each deposit and withdrawal, so that you know the source of each credit and the destination of each debit. This will give you a single document that will provide you with a complete overview of your finances, without the need to match cheque stubs to bills and so on. Buying this book entitles you to

MASTER CASHFLOW ACCOUNT   Record sheet _____   from _____   to _____

Money in

Date	Source	Amount	Balance

Money out

Date	Destination/purpose	Amount	Balance

Balance carried forward to next sheet (Sheet number _____)

Figure 23

photocopy as many copies of this form as you like for your own personal use. Or you may prefer to set up a similar form on a computer spreadsheet.

In step 19 you opened a second current account, and three savings accounts. You will use these to fund four key areas of your life by instructing your bank to transfer set sums to these accounts from your Master Cashflow account. . . .

■ 29 ■

Set up a Monthly Living account

■ Pay your bills automatically.

Name your second current account your Monthly Recurring Living Expense account (or Monthly Living account for short). This account will be used to pay all your fixed living expenses: mortgage/rent, electricity, gas, phone, water, food and so on. Any item which has to be paid every month will be paid from this account.

Most utility companies (gas, electricity, phone, water) offer monthly payment schemes, where your anticipated annual bill is divided into twelve equal payments and you simply pay this amount by standing order every month. These schemes are not only helpful in evening out expenditure (heating bills are otherwise much higher in winter, for example) and automating payment, but also enable you to budget accurately in advance. We recommend that you join these schemes, specifying your Monthly Living account as the account to be debited.

Work out your total monthly living expenses (including shopping), using Figure 24. Obtain the figures from recent bills and bank statements, so that they are accurate rather than optimistic! Leave

Monthly living account – Budget		
Prior.	Item	Amount
	Mortgage/rent	
	Electricity	
	Gas	
	Water	
	Council tax	
	Payments on TV/video/dishwasher/etc.	
	TV licence (a third of quarterly fee)	
	Home and household contents insurance	
	Payments on car loan	
	Car expenses (monthly average)	
	Payments on loans, etc., not listed above	
	Shopping (monthly average)	
	Clothes (monthly average)	
	Household repairs (monthly average)	
	Entertainment (meals out, theatre, etc.)	
	Miscellaneous cash expenditure	
TOTAL MONTHLY EXPENDITURE		

Figure 24

Monthly living account – Options	
Normal monthly expenditure (from above form)	
Reduced expenditure (red and orange items)	
Minimum expenditure (red items only)	

Figure 24 Continued

the 'Priority' column and 'Reduced expenditure' and 'Minimum expenditure' boxes blank for the moment.

The total is the amount to be met from your Monthly Living account. Instruct your bank to transfer this sum from your Master Cashflow account each month. (For two-income families, each transfer your share of the household expenses into your Monthly Living account.) You now have all your normal monthly living expenses automatically funded.

The final stage of this step is to assign a priority to each living expense. This will enable you to identify at a glance expenditure which could be eliminated in an emergency (if your income dropped unexpectedly, for example) or if you simply decided that you wanted to save at the maximum possible rate for a special purchase.

Go through each item, with your partner if you have one, and assign a priority:

- Red for essential.
- Orange for highly desirable but not vital.
- Green for optional.

In other words, red items are those you cannot live without. Orange items are those you would not want to live without, but could if you had to. And green items are the items which are pleasant to have, but you could willingly forgo if you decided you wanted the money for something else.

Add up the totals for red items, and put this figure in the 'Minimum Expenditure' box. Total the orange items, then add in the red total, and put this figure in the 'Reduced Expenditure' box. You now have an at-a-glance guide to the minimum possible amount on which you could survive, and a reduced amount you could live on without too great a sacrifice.

■ 30 ■

Set up a Personal Pleasure account

■ Plan for indulgence.

Name your first savings account your Personal Fun, Entertainment & Pleasure account (or Personal Pleasure account for short). Spending money on pleasure is often one of the first things to go when finances are tight; we argue that it is at these times that it is most important to set aside at least a small amount of money for pure indulgence.

This account has only one rule: it is purely to fund things you want rather than need. It is to pay for meals out, trips to the theatre, films, leisure activities, holidays, weekend breaks . . . anything you like, as long as it is purely for pleasure.

Instruct your bank to transfer a fixed amount into this account from your Master Cashflow account each month. We recommend 5–10 per cent of your income be transferred to this account, more if you can afford it.

Couples should each have their own Personal Pleasure account, with each able to spend their money as and when they choose without comment from the other! This part of the system alone has saved many relationships. . . .

■ 31 ■

Set up a Freedom From Worry account

■ Give yourself peace of mind.

One of the main reasons people give for wanting to be rich is to be free from financial worries. This step will provide you with this freedom from worry even on your existing income.

Name your second savings account your Freedom From Worry account. The purpose of the account is to build up a cushion of money sufficient to meet your living expenses for a minimum of three months. In other words, enough money to fund your Monthly Living account for at least three months.

This account provides peace of mind in two ways. First, if you were to lose your income for any reason, you would know that you had a minimum of three months in which to seek a new source of income, while continuing to enjoy your existing lifestyle. By reducing your expenditure to your Reduced Expenditure or Minimum Expenditure amounts, you can extend this period even further.

Second, you have a reserve fund available to you to meet other emergencies. The account should be used in this way only when absolutely necessary – to 'borrow' from it in other circumstances defeats the object – but you have the reassurance of knowing that it is there if you have no alternative.

Again, instruct your bank to transfer a fixed monthly amount from your Master Cashflow account. We recommend approximately 10 per cent of your income until the account is equal to three month's living expenses, reducing the amount to 5 per cent thereafter.

■ 32 ■

Set up a Financial Independence account

■ The big one.

This is the most ambitious account, but the one which often inspires people more than any of the others. This account is designed to make you financially independent.

Name your third and final savings account your Financial Independence account. The idea of this account is to accumulate funds to the point where the monthly interest on the account is equal to your monthly living expenses. This is our definition of financial independence. At this point, you no longer *need* any other sources of income, and can pick and choose the work you perform.

Since you will not ever withdraw the capital from this account, only the interest, you should upgrade this account to the maximum interest type as soon as the account balance is sufficient to meet the minimum balance requirement. You have the interest credited to the account while it is accumulating and then, once you want to take advantage of it, arrange for the interest to be credited directly to your Monthly Living account.

Although it may appear to take forever to build up sufficient funds to earn the required interest, bear in mind that you are intending to increase your income substantially, and that the account can be useful even when the interest due is less than your monthly expenses. For example, when the interest amounts to half of your monthly expenses, you have the option of reducing your income by half and using the Financial Independence account for the rest.

As with the other accounts, instruct your bank to transfer a fixed monthly amount from your Master Cashflow account. However, we recommend that you supplement this account with lump-sum credits as and when you receive them. You might, for example, decide to pay 50 per cent of any lump-sum payments into this account. If you value financial independence highly, and experience a period during which you earn a substantial amount of money over and above your current needs, you might choose to pay *most* of this money into your Financial Independence account.

To give you an idea of the rate at which your money will grow *from interest alone*, use the 'Rule of 72'. This tells you how long it will take to double your money from compound interest:

- Divide 72 by the annual net interest paid on the account.
- This tells you the number of years required to double your money.

For example, if the account pays 10 per cent interest net, 72 divided by 10 is 7.2, so it will take 7.2 years to double your money purely on the interest earned on a static sum.

■ 33 ■

Set up additional accounts

■ Some other possibilities.

You can use this same principle to fund other areas of your life. Simply set up additional accounts for any other areas of your life you want to fund, and then pay in a fixed monthly amount.

The amount needn't be large – just a few pounds a month will ensure that you have at least some funds available. But, by setting up a standing order from your Master Cashflow account, you ensure that each area is funded automatically and painlessly.

Here are a few examples of accounts set up by people using this system.

■ An Investment account

To ensure you always have money available for unexpected investment opportunities. Many people come across attractive investment opportunities at a time when they don't have sufficient funds to take advantage of them. This account solves the problem.

■ A Sabbatical account

To build up enough money to take a year off every seven years. The idea is to build up at least enough money to cover a year's living expenses, but preferably have additional money available to travel – many people prefer to spend their Sabbatical abroad.

■ A Giving account

To ensure that you always have enough money for gifts.

■ A Tax account

To ensure that you always have enough money to pay your tax bill, if you are responsible for your own taxes. This is a real boon for the self-employed: by paying in the tax element (erring on the side of caution) immediately you receive a payment, you not only free yourself from the worry of the tax bill at the end of each financial year, but you also earn interest on your taxes. We recommend paying the interest, and any surplus as a result of your caution, into your Personal Pleasure account – this can actually have you looking forward to receiving your tax demand!

■ A Travel account

To ensure that you always have money available for spur-of-the-moment weekend breaks, holidays and so on.

Just decide which are the key areas of *your* life, and set up accounts to fund them accordingly.

■ 34 ■

Set up an 'Intangibles' account

■ **Money isn't all that matters.**

Accounts needn't be limited to cash transactions. We also recommend you use a cashbook or computer spreadsheet to create an 'Intangibles' account. This is a place where you can record details of all the non-financial benefits you receive on which you would place a financial value. Figure 25 may be used for this purpose.

Some benefits will be easy to quantify. For example, where you win goods or services in a competition, or take advantage of a free offer of some kind, log the normal cost of the item, or the amount it is worth to you, whichever you prefer. But the range of things which may have financial value to you is much wider than this. For example, if there's a place you've always wanted to visit, and your company (or a client) sends you there on business, you would log the amount the trip would have cost you, or the amount it was worth to you.

Date	Intangible item	Worth

Figure 25

You may even want to take a wider scope than this, and apply a value to a beautiful sunset, an enjoyable walk, a sailing trip, a dinner party with friends ... anything you like. The intention is simply to heighten your appreciation for all forms of value received, and to make it clear that – even using financial value as a measurement – prosperity is not a function of money.

The woman who first used this system reports that she had $300,000 in her 'Intangibles' account within the first four months.

■ 35 ■

Have a purpose for accumulating money

■ Motivate yourself.

We suggested, in step 26, that you assign a purpose for creating money. Something to provide direction, and motivate you through good and bad times alike. We suggest that you do the same for accumulating.

Turn back to step 26 to remind yourself of your purpose for creating money, and to ensure that you remember the distinction between a purpose and goals. Then create a purpose for accumulating money.

For example:

■ To be able to live life spontaneously – decide to do anything at a moment's notice.
■ To be able to spot an opportunity and act immediately.
■ To be able to respond instantly to the needs of my family, friends and favourite causes.

Choose your purpose for accumulating money and write it in the box in Figure 26.

Purpose for accumulating money

Figure 26

■ 36 ■

The secret of enjoyable spending

■ It's what money is for.

Some people will be sorely puzzled by this step. The 'secret' of enjoyable spending? They *love* spending money, and never have any problems enjoying it.

Others, however, usually those good at saving, never fully let themselves enjoy spending money. They spend it carefully, nervously, anxiously, prudently, responsibly, wisely or any one of a dozen other ways, but rarely with relish!

Even people who love money sometimes begrudge spending it, as if the purpose was to accumulate as much as possible and then hold onto it for dear life.

Money has no value when sitting in either a bank account or a shoebox. It has value only when exchanged. Money was specifically *invented* in order to be exchanged. The secret of enjoyable spending is to recognize that spending is what money is *for*. Creating, accumulating, investing . . . these are all steps along the way to spending. None of them are ends in themselves.

The purpose of money is to pass from person to person. To flow. And the faster money passes in and out of our hands, the 'richer' we consider ourselves to be. The difference between someone who earns and spends £10,000 a year and someone who earns and spends a million pounds a year is that the money passes through the hands of the second person at greater speed and in bulkier amounts.

There seems to be a curious, universal phenomenon where spending money is concerned: the way to have money available to spend in a certain way is to spend money in that way.

What do we mean by that? All of us, no matter what our financial circumstances, have at least one item we can *always* find the money for, no matter how broke we may be. It may be feeding our kids. Running a car. Clothes. Meals out with friends. Long phone calls. CDs or tapes. Films or videos. Sailing. Climbing. Holidays. Books. Even if we can't afford anything else, we find money for that one area of our life.

The reason we can always find money for that special area is that we choose to spend money in that area, prioritizing it above everything else. That's the way to have money to spend on something. And the secret of enjoyable spending is to recognize that that's what money is for.

This attitude does require a certain amount of sanity. We're not advocating an approach to life in which you spend money here, there and everywhere, and damn the consequences. That's rarely a recipe for enjoyable spending. But we *are* suggesting that you recognize the purpose of money, and choose to use it for its intended purpose in ways which bring you pleasure and satisfaction. That, when you save, you're saving for a purpose, knowing that the *point* of saving is to have money available for spending.

■ 37 ■

How not to pay your bills

■ And remain within the law.

Most people hate paying bills. Even those who normally enjoy spending money. Which is odd, because the only difference between going on a shopping spree and sitting down to pay the bills is that, with the latter, we already enjoyed the products and services. We had them on a 'try before you buy' deal.

We recommend viewing bills in a new light: voting for what you want in the world.

All commercial organizations are market driven. If large numbers of people buy something, the company will produce more of the same; if insufficient people buy it, the company will cease making the product. Buying something, or, more specifically, *paying for* something, is a way of ensuring that the product or service continues. You are, in effect, voting for the continued production of that item. Or, looking at it in the light of the key to creating money, you are generating agreement for the item.

When you pay your telephone bill, you're voting for more conversations with friends. When you pay your electricity bill, you're voting for music, television, the ability to read at night, tea and coffee, heat, hot meals ... When you pay your water rates you're voting for hot baths, drinks, toilet facilities, cooking....

When you sit down to pay your bills, don't. Instead, use your cheque-book to vote for the things in life you enjoy and want to have available in the future.

Silly? Maybe so, but it's more enjoyable than paying bills.

■ 38 ■

How to enjoy paying taxes

■ Really.

Taxes are like household bills: we tend to view them as a burden rather than an enjoyable and beneficial way to spend our money. We either never see the money in the first place – it's taken from our salary before the money even reaches us – or the largest single cheque we write in the whole year is to the government.

But taxes are like money: we're so used to the concept that we've forgotten that the original intention was to make life easier for us. There are many facilities we take for granted that would barely be possible without taxes. Schools, hospitals, roads, libraries, emergency services, police forces, parks, public transport, consumer protection laws, wild areas protected from development, safety standards, basic income protection ... the list goes on and on. All these are things we have decided, collectively, as the population of a country, that we wish to have available to us. Rather than face the expense and workload of clubbing together in small groups and trying to provide these things, we decided it made more sense to club together as a nation and hire people to organize it all for us. We then each pay a proportion of the costs, and are free to spend our own

Tax-funded expenses you use and/or approve

Figure 27

Tax-funded expenses you use and/or approve

Figure 27 Continued

time in the way we choose, knowing that the services and facilities we value will be provided for us automatically.

Paying tax is like subscribing to a club. A club which provides an enormous number of benefits. As with any other club you join, you may not be interested in – or even approve of – every single benefit or activity provided, but there are sufficient benefits to make the subscription money well spent.

Take a look at the amount of tax you paid last year. Write that amount here:

£_____

Now make a list in Figure 27 of all the things funded by tax which you use and/or approve of.

Make a few phone calls to find out the costs of gaining access to these things privately. For example, if you regularly drive a particular route, work out the mileage and then call a construction company to find out the approximate cost of building a road of this length. Imagine if you had to identify the other people who wanted that particular stretch of road, and then club together between you to have it built. Do this for a few examples from your list. Suddenly our tax bills begin to look like phenomenally good value for money.

Secondly, use your tax liability as an annual guide to your financial status. The higher your tax liability, the better you're doing. This is particularly relevant to those who are self-employed, where gross income may bear no resemblance to actual personal income. Set goals for your tax liability for the next one to ten years.

Finally, if you pay tax annually by cheque, create the tax account suggested in step 33. For each payment you receive, immediately set aside the tax element and pay it into your Tax account. Make it a sum which will definitely cover the tax liability on that payment. At the end of the year, transfer the interest and any surplus into your Personal Pleasure account for a welcome tax-free bonus! Using this system, tax demands hold no fear – you already have the full amount set aside – and you may even find yourself waiting impatiently for your demand so that you can take advantage of the surplus funds.

■ 39 ■

Behave as if you own the world

■ Have the pleasure without the responsibility.

One of the reasons we resent, or at least take no pleasure in, paying taxes is because most of us focus on what we own, rather than what is available to us in the world to enjoy.

There's nothing wrong with taking pleasure in ownership. Most of us have at least one special possession which means a great deal to us, be it something expensive like a home, a plane or a car, or something relatively inexpensive like a special pen, a tennis racquet or a jacket or dress. But there is no reason for us to limit the pleasure we can take in things we *don't* own.

You may not own a mountain, but you can take as much pleasure in gazing at it as the person who does. You may not own a collection of paintings in an art gallery, but you can take as much pleasure in looking at them as the person who does. Conversely, you may own a watch, but – if a thief steals it – you can't tell the time, while the thief can. Ownership is an invented concept. Babies don't own anything, but enjoy everything. They don't care whether or not they own a dummy or a pram or a toy: they don't allow their enjoyment to be limited by thoughts of ownership. Like the other invented concepts discussed in other steps, money and taxes, for example, ownership is a useful concept, but it becomes counter-productive if we allow it to limit our enjoyment of life.

Make two lists in Figure 28. On the left, things you own. On the right, things you enjoy whether or not you own them. Neither list need be comprehensive, just aim for a good sample of about 20–40 items in each list. If you find a good deal of overlap in the two lists, look specifically for examples of things you enjoy but do not own.

We suggest enjoying everything you use as if it were yours. If you walk through a shop, do so as if it were yours (please note that even the owner of the store will pay for anything they remove from the store!). If you hire a car, take as much pleasure in driving it as if you owned it. When you travel, enjoy the flight and the hotel as much as if you owned both the airline and hotel chain. When you walk through some beautiful countryside, treat it as your own land (as a caring owner).

In fact, *not* owning something sometimes gives you a better deal – you can enjoy the walk through the countryside without worrying about rebuilding the fences, stay in the hotel without worrying about paying the city taxes, drive the hire car without worrying about the repair bill in case of mechanical failure, and so on. There is tremendous freedom in having the pleasure without the responsibility.

One of the implications of acting as if you owned everything is that it becomes natural to ask for precisely what you want. If you would prefer a different hotel room, you would ask for it if you owned the hotel. If you owned the art gallery, you would ask your staff to tell you anything you wanted to know about a particular painting. We recommend being a charming owner. The sort of owner who always couches everything in the form of a charming request, and is perfectly willing to hear that something is not possible (you want

Things I own	Things I enjoy

Figure 28

your staff to take care of your business as well as cater to you, after all), but nevertheless doesn't hesitate to ask for what he or she wants.

■ 40 ■

The secrets of successful investment

■ Three simple secrets.

Like the secret of successful saving, the secrets of successful investment are simple:

■ Invest in what you love.

If you love fine paintings, buy those. If you love exciting new business ventures, invest in those. If you are committed to environmental issues, invest in some form of green technology. If you want to work for the end of world hunger, invest in small businesses in developing countries. If you love high technology, invest in that. If you adore antiques, invest in those. Find something you love, or are passionate about, and then invest in that.

This is a pragmatic basis for investment: we tend to become most knowledgeable about those subjects which most interest us. And the more we know about something, the better chance we have of investing successfully in it.

At best, you'll make a lot of money. At worst, you'll lose money while surrounding yourself with things you love or contributing to something you hold dear.

- Don't put all your eggs in one basket.
- Don't invest what you can't afford to lose.

Never forget that 'investing' is a respectable word for 'gambling.' There are no guarantees, and no such thing as a 'foolproof scheme' or 'safe bet'. The most successful investments multiply their value by thousands of per cent, the least successful lose every penny.

Always spread your risk across several investments, so that if one fails totally you will never lose everything, and never, never invest money you can't afford to lose. If you need to be sure of maintaining the value of your capital, put it in a savings account with a large bank or buy government bonds. Save the speculative investments for money you can afford to lose.

■ 41 ■

Managing your investments

■ Reap the rewards.

There is one additional secret to successful investing which some-times escapes even those with impeccable investment records: reaping the rewards.

Some people are extremely good at accumulating capital, but much less skilled at taking advantage of their success. We suggest splitting the proceeds of a successful investment as follows. Reinvest half, to enable you to continue building on your success, and split the balance three ways:

- ■ To your Investment account.
- ■ To your Financial Independence account.
- ■ To your Personal Pleasure account.

Placing some of the proceeds into your Investment account ensures that you spread the risk by diversifying into other investments, and gives you the means to repeat your success in future.

Investment payoffs are one of the best ways to build up your Financial Independence account as quickly as possible, and is the perfect place to put money if you have ambitions about earning your living from your investments – the Financial Independence account will act as your safety net.

Finally, always put some of the money into your Personal Pleasure account so that you enjoy the fruits of your success in the present as well as in the future.

■ 42 ■

The nine keys to prosperity

■ The basis of the book.

There are nine key principles behind the programme described in this book. We suggest that you copy this step and put it on your wall, in your organizer or somewhere else where you will constantly be reminded of it.

■ 1 Find out what you love to do, and do it

People make good livings from the unlikeliest activities. They are no different from you or me. We spend more time working than in any other waking activity: it is crazy to do something you don't enjoy. Choose something, and create a living doing it.

Remember that even people who love what they do have days when they are bored, doubtful, stressed. . . . Once you have chosen what it is you want to do, don't be put off by fleeting feelings.

■ 2   Live in the present

Enjoy the present, even when working for the future. Remember that money won't buy the key quality you seek, even though we all think it will. Be present to that quality now.

■ 3   Be true to yourself

Honesty and integrity are a source of prosperity; without them, it is possible to be rich, but not prosperous. Don't sacrifice prosperity for wealth.

■ 4   Be willing to start again

You may be financially successful doing something you hate. What you do now may have excited you once, but now bores you. Be willing to start from scratch. Find something you love now. Don't die doing something you no longer enjoy merely because you're good at it.

■ 5   Contribute

Contribution is an essential element of prosperity. People often put off contributing their time, money or abilities, intending to do it once they have enough time, enough money, enough ability. The way to have enough of something is to start giving it.

■ 6   Be willing to be wrong

Many people would rather be right and poor than wrong and rich. Remember that most of your thoughts, opinions, beliefs, rules, attitudes and philosophies aren't even your own. Be true to your core values, not a slave to your upbringing.

■ 7   Be committed to yourself and your goals

Commitment is not measured by a sincere tone of voice, a fierce look in your eye or the passion with which you make your case. Commitment is measured by the consistency of your actions over time. Commitment is tested only when the going gets tough. Be flexible in your approach, but remain committed to your goals.

■ 8   Work for your purpose

Keep in mind the purpose you chose for creating and accumulating money. Ensure that your actions are consistent with your purpose. Ensure that your purpose governs the goals you set yourself.

■ 9   Have fun with money

Remember that money is a game. The goal is to win, but the purpose is to enjoy playing.

Now that you have finished reading the book and have done the exercises, we are very interested in your comments or feedback.

If you would like to write to us, you may do so at:

Time & Money
235 Whitney Street
San Francisco
California 94131
United States of America

We would also like you to know about two courses, which Paul de Haas has been leading all over the world. If you would like to be notified when these courses are scheduled to be held in your area, please complete and return the form on the following page.

The Money Course
An Introduction to Power over Money

promises

1. You will be more able and successful in the four areas of money and wealth. The areas are:
   - (a) Earning
   - (b) Saving
   - (c) Spending
   - (d) Investing
2. You will find out the truth about all financial problems, including your own, and be given the technology to resolve them.
3. You will receive real, practical tools and strategies to maximize the results of your financial dealings.
4. You will generate a new 'paradigm' from which to operate in the area of money and wealth; one which gives access to having money become not an object, but a powerful edge in living; a tool for fulfilling actions and achieving ends that are aligned with your real intentions in life.

The Money Course takes place over two 5-hour sessions, usually a week apart and usually scheduled in the evenings from h.18:00–h.23:00.

The Time Course
Access to a Powerful Future

The Time Course promises . . .

An opportunity to learn and master a new way of seeing and organizing your life so that you have:

- Less stress, effort and worry
- Less time wasted
- More results, accomplishments and fun
- An empowered sense of purpose and direction
- More time for family, friends and community
- More time for your personal well-being

The Time Course not only provides the structure for greater productivity, but also the tools to make that structure a part of your daily life. The Time Book is a complete personal management system, which is the result of ten years of refinement based on the input from thousands of course participants. If you view The Time Course as a blueprint for productivity, The Time Book provides the structure and tools to achieve results. Every participant in The Time Course will receive The Time Book.

The Time Course takes place on one full day from h.09:00–h.18:00 followed by a 3-hour session usually two days later from h.19:00–h.22:00.

If you would like to be notified about scheduled courses please tick the appropriate box(es).

☐ Please notify me when there is a Money Course scheduled in my area.
☐ Please notify me when there is a Time Course scheduled in my area.

Your name: _____

Address: _____

_____

_____

Mail this page (or photocopy of it) to:

Time & Money
235 Whitney Street
San Francisco
California 94131
United States of America